HUMPTY Dumpty

Flip-Side Rhymes

FROM the
perspective of
HUMPTY DUMPTY

by christopher Harbo

illustrated by Danny chatzikonstantinou

PICTURE WINDOW BOOKS
a capstone imprint

Humpty Dumpty

sat on a wall,

Humpty
Dumpty
had a
great fall.

All the king's horses

and all the king's men

couldn't put Humpty together again.

NOW FLIP THE BOOK
TO GET ANOTHER SIDE OF THE RHYME.

Editor: Gillia Olson
Designer: Ashlee Suker
Art Director: Nathan Gassman
Production Specialist: Laura Manthe
The illustrations in this book were created digitally.

Picture Window Books are published by Capstone.
1710 Roe Crest Drive, North Mankato, Minnesota 56003
www.capstoneyoungreaders.com

Library of Congress Cataloging-in-Publication Data

Harbo, Christopher L.
Humpty Dumpty flip-side rhymes / by Christopher Harbo ; illustrated by Danny Chatzikonstantinou.
   pages cm. — (Nonfiction picture books. Flip-side nursery rhymes)
   Summary: "Color illustrations and simple text give the original Humpty Dumpty nursery rhyme, along with a fractured version from the perspective of the king's men"— Provided by publisher.
   ISBN 978-1-4795-6006-6 (paper over board)
   ISBN 978-1-4795-6984-7 (ebook PDF)
   1. Nursery rhymes. 2. Children's poetry. 3. Upside-down books—Specimens. [1. Nursery rhymes. 2. Upside-down books.] I. Chatzikonstantinou, Danny, illustrator. II. Mother Goose. III. Title.
   PZ8.3.H19669Hu 2015
   398.2—dc23   2014032214
                                              [E]

Printed in the United States of America in North Mankato, Minnesota.
092014   008482CGS15

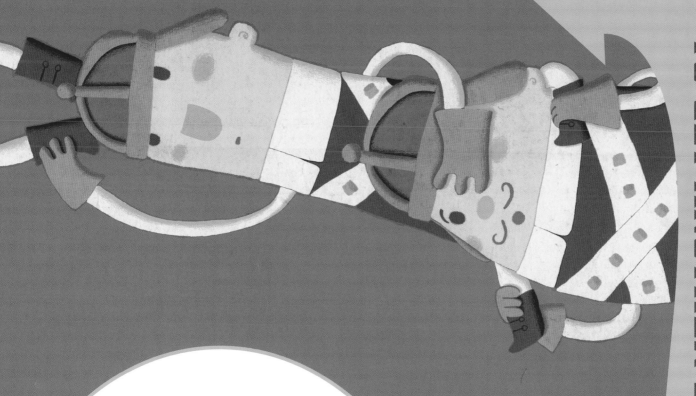

NOW **FLIP** THE BOOK
TO GET ANOTHER SIDE OF THE RHYME.

other titles in this series:

JACK and **Jill**
Flip-Side Rhymes

Little **BO** **PEEP**
Flip-Side Rhymes

Little **MUFFET**
Flip-Side Rhymes

So the men ate
a breakfast

and off their steeds rambled.

They threw up their hands

And gluing the pieces together caused fits.

Humpty broken to bits.

men found

The king's

2

HUMPTY
Dumpty

FLiP-Side
Rhymes

FROM the Perspective
of the KING'S MEN

by Christopher Harbo

illustrated by Danny Chatzikonstantinou

PICTURE WINDOW BOOKS
a capstone imprint